THE SECOND PETER PRINCIPLE

Richard A. Hamilton

First Printing, December 1991

International Standard Book Number
0-88290-428-0

Horizon Publishers' Catalog and Order Number
1039

Printed and distributed
in the United States of America by

Horizon Publishers
& Distributors, Incorporated
P.O. Box 490 Bountiful, Utah 84011-0490

DEDICATION

To my wife Helga, who truly made
this book possible.

May I repay her by living
up to what I have written.

And

To Denzel Wiser,
who challenged
me
to understand.

CONTENTS

1
Introduction

The biggest mistake I ever made was to be unhappy. Much of my life has been spent facing an unresolved conflict. I have always had a heroic vision of man—an idea that he really was made in the image of God.

The conflict came when I looked—really looked—at myself and those around me. I could see the pettiness and the laziness and the myriads of seemingly unconquerable flaws in us all. I was not what I wanted to be, and my efforts to modify self had not met with anything approximating dramatic success.

I was nearly at the point of ignoring, as best as I could, the entire issue when I happened upon a particularly relevant several pages in the Autobiography of Benjamin Franklin. At the age of twenty-two, Franklin, "*. . . conceiv'd the bold and arduous project of arriving at moral perfection.*"

Franklin continued, *"I wish'd to live without committing any fault at any time; I would conquer all that either natural inclination, custom, or company might lead me into. As I knew, or thought I knew, what was right and wrong, I did not see why I might not always do the one and avoid the other."*

Franklin then proceeded to outline a methodical approach to the attainment of his goal. This, I thought, was exactly what I had been looking for! Man is made in the image of God. And man is what he is simply because he doesn't know how to change his situation.

A few paragraphs later, however, Franklin continued, "*. . . I* *soon found I had undertaken a task of more difficulty than I had imagined. While my care was employ'd in guarding against one fault, I was often surprised by another; habit took the advantage of inattention; inclination was sometimes too strong for reason. I concluded, at length, that the mere speculative conviction that it was our interest to be completely virtuous, was not sufficient to prevent our slipping . . .*"

Franklin adhered to his plan for most of his life. Six years before his death, he wrote, *"I enter'd upon the execution of this plan . . . and continu'd it with occasional intermissions for some time. I was surpris'd to find myself so much fuller of faults than I had imagined; but I had the satisfaction of seeing them diminish."*

Franklin's disclosure that his system really had not produced the moral perfection that he sought was a blow to the enthusiasm and excitement that I had experienced a few pages earlier. Still, there might be a workable modification . . . .

Some time later, a friend challenged me to really come to an understanding of a few verses in the first chapter of the Second Epistle of Peter. *The Second Peter Principle* develops that understanding—and combines it with the attempts of Benjamin Franklin to develop a system that does lead to "moral perfection"—and beyond.

Like Franklin, I too must report that I have not yet achieved "moral perfection." Unlike Franklin, I have a reasonable confidence that I will succeed.

As for unhappiness, *The Second Peter Principle* has taught me that discontent is the product of limited vision and stagnation. Even more important is the realization that happiness is merely a poor reflection of the more transcendent state—that of joy. Application of *The Second Peter Principle* brings all of this—and more—into your life.

* * *

By way of explanation at this point, I would observe that I lay no claim to being a scriptural authority, doctrinal scholar, or of having any other such title that a doubtful reader might wish either to ascribe to me—or to strip from me. I can say only that I have read the scriptures at least once a year for the last dozen or so years. I have read several commentaries at the same time.

In the final analysis I think that I have studied somewhat "critically" in the sense of seeking to find any and all doctrines within the context of a coherent whole—and to recog nize "truth" within the same context. I encourage all who might read any of the following to, likewise, read critically and to judge for themselves.

* * *

One last set of introductory comments: speaking of moral perfection raises the possible spectre of sectarian religious discussions. That is not my intention. Again, I would like to use a few of Franklin's words to help set the tone. Franklin sought to identify a commonality of belief. He did so in these words:

> *"That there is one God, who*
> *made all things.*
> *"That he governs the world*
> *by his providence,*
> *"That he ought to be worshiped*
> *by adoration, prayer, and thanksgiving.*
> *"But that the most acceptable*
> *service of God is doing good to man.*
> *"That the soul is immortal.*
> *"And that God will certainly reward*
> *virtue and punish vice, either here*
> *or hereafter."*

Ben Franklin was a man of faith, a seeker of truth, a seeker of a better self—and a man who had little patience for sectarian squabbles. May this book proceed in the same spirit.

2
Moral Perfection

"Moral perfection is like pornography," claims a friend of mine, *"I may not be able to define it, but I know it when I see it."*

Many people see things differently. For instance, I remember a preacher I once had. More accurately, he was a preacher my parents once had. His idea of moral perfection seemed to require a wardrobe of sackcloth and ashes, a diet of locusts and honey (with emphasis being given to the former), an eternally somber countenance—with *no* room for humor, and a dedication to the idea that, if I were to marry, I was to limit conjugal relations to the absolute minimum necessary for procreation.

There was more to it than that, but those were the relevant highlights that stuck in the mind of a sixteen-year-old boy. More than thirty years have since passed, and I can no more accept that notion now than I could then.

As I reflect back on those discussions, I can now see that my opposition was more instinctive than reasoned. Today, I would still disagree with him, but my current opposition would be that his concept was based entirely on the outward appearance—and that it had nothing at all to do with the quality of the inner man. This reminds me of a book entitled *The Mask of Sanity.* This book is about sociopaths and psychopaths—individuals whose behavior is so outrageous and anti-social that they, themselves, must erect a facade of normalcy, a mask of sanity in order to survive. Likewise, my preacher friend was creating only his own particular facade for the world—his own mask of piety.

My interest then, my interest now, is to do away with the pretense, to eliminate the facade—and to get to the heart of the matter. In the intervening years, I have encountered other ideas that have attempted to equate moral perfection with that which is most pleasing and satisfying to man—i.e., the idea that, "If it feels good, do it."

I knew that wasn't it either. Such an approach is like inspecting an entire length of chain and, when discovering the weakest link, re-writing the specifications to say, in effect, "this is the best we can do"—thereby ignoring the evidence of all of the other links that were obviously stronger.

In these same years I have been fortunate to have known a number of individuals who had a tangible uniqueness about them—men who possessed a special quality, purpose, and approach that seemed inseparably associated with a clear sense that they had achieved, or at least were approaching, this thing called moral perfection.

It may be true that the real miracle is not so much in the meeting of such individuals as it is in the recognizing them. We live in a world where polite conventions require that we not discuss "controversial" topics such as religion and politics. Too often, such discussions are acrimonious; too often they end with offense having been given—and taken. Yet these are the kinds of issues that shape our lives—that give strength and dimension to who we really are. These are the few issues really worth discussing.

This brings me back to those whom I have met who appear to be approaching moral perfection. Each of them seems to have a special talent for discussing such topics without rancor and without giving offense. I might have substantial initial disagreement with their conclusions; but, in general, there is an honest respect for their positions. And, in a personal sense, I have discovered that I have often, ultimately, changed my own perceptions and have come to share their same conclusions—with my often having learned a great principle in the process.

In short, I am suggesting that there is great power associated with moral perfection. It may even be a part of a precise definition of the term. It is the power that comes from the recognition of universal and enduring truths. It is the power that comes from a respect for the potential of all men to achieve perfection.

But, rather than rely forever on the words of my friend, who "... knows it when he sees it," let me suggest that Paul, in one of his exhortations to the Romans, comes close to identifying that special quality of spirit that comes with "moral perfection." He wrote,

> *Let love be without dissimulation.*
> *Abhor that which is evil; cleave to that*
> *which is good.*
> *Be kindly affectioned one to another*
> *with brotherly love; in honor preferring*
> *one another;*
> *Not slothful in business; fervent in*
> *spirit; serving the Lord;*
> *Rejoicing in hope; patient in*
> *tribulation; continuing instant in prayer;*
> *Distributing to the necessity of*
> *saints; given to hospitality.*
> *Bless them which persecute you:*
> *bless and curse not.*
> *Rejoice with them that do rejoice, and*
> *weep with them that weep.*
> *Be of the same mind one toward*
> *another. Mind not high things, but*
> *condescend to men of low estate. Be not*
> *wise in your own conceits.*
> *Recompense to no man evil for evil.*
> *Provide things honest in the sight of*
> *all men.*
> *If it be possible, as much as lieth*
> *in you, live peaceably with all men.*
> *Dearly beloved, avenge not yourselves,*

but rather give place unto wrath: for it is written, Vengeance is mine; I will repay, saith the Lord.

Therefore, if thine enemy hunger, feed him; if he thirst, give him drink: for in so doing thou shalt heap coals of fire on his head.

Be not overcome of evil, but overcome evil with good.

Romans 12:9-21

When we choose to look at ourselves with honesty—when we see the myriad of little things that we do not like, the problem of achieving personal perfection is the seeming impossibility of the task. We may be properly embarked upon changing some aspect of our life when along comes a new, and apparently more formidable flaw which, obviously, must be dealt with at once. The original fault is now relegated to a position of lesser importance, and is usually soon forgotten in the press of more immediate concerns.

If it were only one thing that we had to conquer, if it were only one of those verses from Paul that we had to live up to, then, of course, each of us could do it. But, there is so much . . . .

Rather than be debilitated by the seeming impossibility of the task, it is now time to add another dimension to our definition of perfection. This time, from Webster, we learn that perfection is "the act or process of perfecting." True, it can also mean a state of being that is absolute. However, it must be remembered that it is also a process. What is required, what is truly self-satisfying, is the *honest* knowledge that we are doing, diligently, all that we can.

There is an orderly approach to the process. It is an approach that is more orderly and more profoundly logical than that followed by Benjamin Franklin. It is an approach that does not waste time on the non-essentials. It is *The Second Peter Principle.*

3
The Peter Principle

In 1969, Dr Laurence J. Peter made a series of observations in a little book entitled, *The Peter Principle.* The actual stated principle he formulated is, *"In a Hierarchy Every Employee Tends to Rise to His Level of Incompetence."*

That logic, carried to its ultimate conclusion, says that man, himself, sooner or later must reach his level of life incompetence. In fact, Dr. Peter came to that same conclusion.

I am not here to disagree with the validity of Dr. Peter's observations. In reality, I could add a long litany of complaints and observations that might seem to support his thesis.

We do live in a time when anything approximating a heroic vision of man seems to be virtually non-existent. We have come to accept as commonplace almost everything that is mundane, mediocre, glib, superficial, opportunistic, unethical (if not outright illegal), and profane (or more often, explicitly crude and vulgar). Worse, it seems as if we are coming to accept this as the best that we can hope for from ourselves. Such acceptance, however, is a matter of choice and a matter of perception.

Dr. Peter has identified the weakest link in the chain, and he has formulated a "principle" around it. At the moment, he may even be right when it comes to "me." I may be an incompetent, bumbling, crude, opportunistic and amoral oaf.

But, no "principle" says that I must remain so. I do not need his help in identifying the weakest in me. I know these flaws better than anyone else. More important to me is the strongest link in the chain, and the fires that forged and strengthened it. By identifying strength, and by duplicating the processes that produced it, I shall transcend incompetence.

4
The Second Peter Principle

Nearly two thousand years ago a simple Galilean fisherman set down on paper, parchment, or whatever a conditional promise—and a formula whereby the promise might be fulfilled.

The promise, simply put, was that, ". . . *Ye might be partakers of the divine nature.*"

In this profound commitment, I was promised that I could push beyond my personal frontiers of limited competence. I could transcend incompetence. I *could* achieve the condition described by Paul. This is the promise of *The Second Peter Principle, ". . . Ye might be partakers of the divine nature.*"

I also contemplated who it was that was making this promise. Peter was a simple man. He had some substantial weaknesses. (If you remember, Peter was the one who denied his master three times.)

When I look at myself; when I am honest enough to strip away all of my facades, I too am a simple man. With some substantial weaknesses.

So, when Peter makes such a promise, I have a reasonable hope that I can realize its fulfillment. (Besides, I can also identify with a fisherman that needs divine intervention in order to catch a decent fish!)

Anyhow, the promise was made, and I came to believe it. The next step was to understand the conditions. The promise, and the conditions as given by Peter, follow:

Whereby are given unto us exceeding great and precious promises: that by these ye might be partakers of the divine nature, having escaped the corruption that is in the world through lust.

And beside this, giving all diligence, add to your faith virtue; and to virtue knowledge;

And to knowledge temperance; and to temperance patience; and to patience godliness;

And to godliness brotherly kindness; and to brotherly kindness charity.

For if these things be in you and abound, they make you that ye shall neither be barren nor unfruitful in the knowledge of our Lord Jesus Christ.

But he that lacketh these things is blind, and cannot see afar off, and hath forgotten that he was purged from his old sins,

Wherefore the rather, brethren, give diligence to making your calling and election sure: for if ye do these things, ye shall never fall:

For so an entrance shall be ministered unto you abundantly into the everlasting kingdom of our Lord and Savior Jesus Christ.

II Peter 1:4-11

I do not know how many times I have read these words. I do know that I have been consistently struck with a sense that they contained the "secret" of how I was to accomplish the same thing that Ben Franklin set out to accomplish. But understanding has come slowly.

Clearly, there is a sequential relationship that is defined:

1. Escape the corruption of the world.
2. Have faith.
3. Add virtue.
4. Add knowledge.
5. Add temperance.
6. Add patience.
7. Add godliness.
8. Add brotherly kindness.
9. Add charity.

And, do it all diligently.

At first glance, it does make a kind of sense. I have known a number of people who discovered religion and who wished to instantly get to the finish line and have charity which they understood to be the pure love of Christ.

Somehow, however, they never seemed to be quite credible when they lost patience with their teen-aged children—or when they rejoiced at having found a new tax loophole. For them it was like building a castle in the air without a foundation. Clearly some things come first as a part of that necessary foundation.

But, what are the specific relationships that say that one virtue or characteristic must precede another? And, just what do some of these terms really mean?

5
Escape the Corruption of the World

The road to moral perfection, or charity, as Peter would have it, is a spiritual one. To get onto that road requires a number of conscious decisions. A spiritual road is similar to the roads and freeways we are used to in our temporal lives. The inter-state system that connects our cities and states has limits, laws, conventions, and sometimes tolls governing its use and access.

Judging from my observations, most of those limits, laws and conventions are regularly ignored by a population that has a good local knowledge of the limits to which they can go with at least a measure of impunity. But even if we ignore those laws, we are at least comfortable in knowing that they are there.

I suggest that spiritual roads are very much like that. There are laws and limits, although of a different nature. The signs aren't posted as often. And while there are "speed traps" as it were, the ultimate accountability is usually deferred for years. Although, some would attempt to maintain that there will never be any accountability at all.

In any case, the world in which we live can be fairly described as a self-centered, hedonistic, and humanistic enterprise. Taking any kind of a turn away from that usually sets us at some variance with our neighbors. That is usually an uncomfortable position.

Let me give you an example. Some years ago I was employed by a fish processing company. I do not know if that company was typical of its industry. I prefer to believe that it was not. However, for a discussion of corruption in the world, that company is a good place to start.

While employed there, I had a very bright young man working for me. He was well educated, sharp, aggressive, and hard working. He had a beautiful wife and a small child. He had a marriage which he described as "open"—meaning that he and his wife had decided not to be confined by the conventional, monogamous, "restrictive" covenants of an "up-tight" and puritanical society. He tried to make it sound good. But there were two problems. Every time that he availed himself of his "freedom," he would come to work the following day—sometimes with a hang-over—but always with a consuming depression approaching, almost, remorse. The only days that were worse for him were those days following his wife's telling him of her "openness."

I am not proud to report that this young man and I never developed much of a friendship. I did not approve of his life-style; I never really said much about it. However, he did have a friend in the company whom he did respect. That friend, like many others in the firm, had behaved similarly for years. But, one day the friend came to a realization that he was destroying himself and his family—everything that was really important to him. Literally overnight, he changed. That change cost him the friendship of the young man who worked for me. My employee viewed his friend's change as a moral judgment upon himself—a repudiation of his free and open life-style. (In reality, it was!)

It is an interesting aside for me to also observe that such conduct was commonplace within the company; and it was not a surprise for me to read, several years after I had changed employment, that the company went into bankruptcy amidst wide-spread charges of fraud. Compromising integrity in one area of one's life obviously makes corollary compromises in other areas just that much easier.

For most of us, choosing to escape the corruption of the world is not so dramatic as the renouncing of adultery. It is the myriad of little things that we turn away from—and, in the aggregate, find much strength and discipline in the turning-away process.

In fact there are practices of several religions that make much sense in this regard. Jews have a strict set of dietary laws. A case might be made that there were once strong health considerations favoring such dietary restrictions. However, it would take a very brave person to argue the continuation of those laws on that basis today.

Yet, they remain good laws. They set Jews apart from the rest of society in a small, harmless, yet significant way. Society did not need the reminder. But, Jewish people did—and do. The strength of these laws was to remind themselves on a daily basis that they were different—that they had, in effect, made a covenant to escape the corruption of the world. This was a reminder, and at the same time an exercise that strengthened them, that built discipline for those times when more substantial challenges would be posed.

Until several years ago, Catholics did not eat meat on Fridays and certain other days. Likewise, they set themselves apart—and were strengthened. (It is interesting also to note the apparent weakening of Catholic unity, harmony, and personal discipline in the years following the abandonment of that practice.)

Mormons don't smoke, drink coffee or anything stronger for the same basic reason. Such little acts are the least—yet most basic steps that must be taken as one sets out to travel a spiritual path towards growth and perfection.

As for the relationship to faith, it seems self-evident that much of the world knows only that which it can see, hear, touch, taste, smell, or feel. Given that, the world knows nothing of the Spirit. Hence, to know the Spirit, pieces of the world must be rejected, corruption must be escaped, and supplanted with something more.

However, before advancing to a discussion of that next step, there is one more important element of "escaping the corruption of the world" to be considered. Escaping corruption is not just a one-time, "do it and be done" sort of exercise. Rather, it is a step which must be repeated with some frequency.

I must also tell you that the first time that I had to "go back to square one," as it were, I was almost devastated. I had been working through the steps of *The Second Peter Principle*—and I felt that I was really making some headway in the remodeling of "me." But, with the sudden and acute awareness that there was an unmistakable element of the world that I had to set behind me, I was assailed with the feelings that I was doing it all wrong—that my time had been wasted and that I had gotten nowhere.

Such misguided feelings of depression and frustration are probably the biggest barrier to achieving the goal of a perfected self. Certainly, such feelings do not square with the realities of the process.

The steps of adding virtue, of adding knowledge, of adding temperance will inevitably reveal worldly practices and attitudes that are self-destructive and that are in direct opposition to the very things that you are attempting to accomplish.

With that realization, there comes a change in attitude. It becomes less and less a matter of "giving something up." It becomes less and less of a sacrifice. It becomes more truly an "escape"—an escape from a literal bondage. Consider the word "escape" and our usage of it. We never "escape" from something or someplace that we truly enjoy. For example, a party and the attendant associations that I would have enjoyed six months or a year ago, might, today, be an event from which I most earnestly desire to escape.

As the process of perfection proceeds, so will your perceptions of escaping the corruption of the world. It becomes less and less something that you have to do. It becomes, with greater maturity, more like something that you get to do. It is a reward. It is something like the game of Monopoly. Every time you get back to the beginning of the board, you are rewarded.

It might also be likened to a perception of John the Baptist. One perception of him could easily be that here was a man who had given up everything—wandering in the desert, wearing a crude camel's hair garment and surviving on locusts and honey. A more knowledgeable perception of him, however, might remember that today we would pay a premium for a camel's hair coat or blazer—prizing its softness and durability. Knowledge might also reveal to us that the locust tree (prevalent in the area) is also known as the carob—a tree that produces a chocolate substitute. With this in mind, it is easy to see John as one who truly enjoyed the finer things in life, and had a sweet tooth as well.

Truly, following *The Second Peter Principle* will change perceptions. Escaping the corruption that is in the world will inevitably lead to the destination of all escapes—to freedom.

6
Faith

In seeking to offer a definition for "faith," an observation made by Tolstoy comes to mind. The world would look at a biographical sketch of Leo Tolstoy—and conclude that by any standards, he was a success. He was a brilliant novelist with a great talent that went beyond not only the borders of his country, but also the time in which he lived. He achieved fame in his own time. With the fame came wealth and position. He loved and was satisfied with his family.

He was also, for much of his life, a dedicated student in many different disciplines. Yet, the meaning of life itself escaped him for years. Lacking that understanding, he could not view himself as a success. He sought diligently for understanding. Finally, at the point of despair, he came to realize that *"Faith is the force of life."*

Man is distinguished from the lower animals by his ability to think and to reason. He is also distinguished by his ability to choose not to use the intellect that he has been given. With intelligence has also come agency—the ability to choose and select among varying courses of action.

If my life is the least bit typical, I can report that it has all too often been the case that the choices that I have made have been the easy ones. It is easy to be intellectually lazy—to accept the simple answers.

Intellect and reason set man apart from the lower animals. Is there anything else that particularly distinguishes man? For too long I neglected consideration of this very basic question. But, once asked, understanding began to flow.

Free agency sets us apart. We truly do have the ability to make "rational choices."

We also have emotions. There are many who might not view this as a particularly positive distinction. In fact, the adjective "emotional" has, in general usage, acquired a negative connotation. But, think it through! The most worthwhile moments in life are the emotional ones. Every now and again we may be privileged to experience those moments of transcendent joy that cause all past griefs to melt in insignificance. Joy, love, happiness, satisfaction, grief, sorrow, desolation, despair, even hatred—all of these add dimension to the spirit, to that which is really "me."

In an additional defense of "emotion," I would also observe that those attributes of God that we find most comforting are those that we associate with his emotional state. He is kind, loving, compassionate, and forgiving. Even when he is vengeful, it is in a perfectly just and righteous sense.

Closely akin to all of this is "faith." As Tolstoy said, "Faith is the force of life." Reason may be the means by which I make "rational" choices. Faith is the means by which I make choices of the "spirit"—and the means by which I temper (ie, make stronger) my "rational" choices.

The Apostle Paul offered a simple definition of faith as, *". . . the substance of things hoped for: the evidence of things not seen."* If faith is, in fact, "substance" and "evidence"—and even of sufficient strength to modify "rational" choices, then it must follow that faith is inseparably connected with those concepts that we call truth and knowledge.

Understanding the process whereby faith develops and grows will perhaps clarify the links between faith, truth, and knowledge.

Faith begins with a simple idea. That idea is that God actually exists, that he has certain attributes, that he has certain expectations of us, and that we will ultimately be held accountable for what we have, or have not, done.

No man starts this process having a comprehensive and accurate idea as to the exact nature and attributes of God. That understanding comes, step by step, precept by precept—and sometimes painfully.

Picture, in a hypothetical example, three young men who have come together to run a race. Each of these young men is equal in his understanding (or his lack of understanding) of God. Each is equal in faith. They are unequal in physical ability. Yet, all three, prior to the race, offer up a fervent prayer that they might be the winner of the race. The race is run, and by definition, there must be two losers.

One loser may conclude that his faith was not rewarded, that God was not just, or that God was not capable of influencing the outcome of the race—or, that there really wasn't a God in the first place.

The other loser might make the reasonable observation that all races are not equal, and that the more appropriate prayer to have been offered would have sought divine assistance in running the best race that he was capable of. In coming to this conclusion, this young man will have added to his understanding of the true nature of things, and he will build from there.

The winner of the race has won only the race. His lesson has only been deferred; it is inevitable that he will meet a better runner than himself. And from that point he, like the two losers, will either grow or not.

There is a starting point in these understandings with which most reasonable men would agree, irrespective of potential secular differences. First of all, God is the same today as he was yesterday, and as he will be tomorrow. He is not a respecter of persons. And those concepts that we label as truth, justice, love, mercy, faith, power, knowledge—all find their standard of perfection resting with him.

Using this as a starting point, I would offer a personal guide for considering something that is purportedly an attribute or characteristic of God. That is to simply ask the question, "Is it believable?"

This little test may seem naive, but let me illustrate. Martin Luther, in speaking of a doctrinal proposition that was as incomprehensible to him as it is to me, said, *"I know that it is incomprehensible and unbelievable; yet, it is a measure of the strength of my faith that I do believe it."*

At the risk of appearing irreverent to my Lutheran friends, I suggest that this cannot be faith. To accept Luther's statement requires a complete disassociation of faith from truth and knowledge. More fundamentally, we would have to change our basic concept of God. If faith is a foundation, a first principle, a commandment to believe (and it is), then a commandment to believe in the unbelievable necessarily conjures up the image of a capricious and changeable God. Hence, the question, "Is it believable?" is a valid test.

Finally, I would make a few observations about the effects of faith. The most important effect of faith is that it is the cause of action. Faith plants a seed. Faith opens and maintains a savings account. Faith is the motive force behind all acts that anticipate future benefit.

Faith, therefore, is power. It is the power to change self. It is the power to influence others for good.

To illustrate, I would tell you a story related by a powerful teacher. He is one of the most productive men in our society. He is an educator. He is an accomplished author. He is a consultant to many of the "Fortune 500" companies—teaching their top executives basic principles of motivation.

He tells of an experience with his own son where the application of the principles that he was teaching had no apparent force and effect.

The son was succumbing to many of the temptations and destructive practices of the so-called "me generation." Such behavior was in direct opposition to everything that the father believed and presumably practiced. With great love and concern, the father embraced the boy and encouraged and applauded all that he perceived as "right" behavior—and expressed disappointment with the "wrong" behavior. The father did all that he taught his corporate clients to do. The son's pursuit of self-destructive activities was all the more rapid.

In desperation, that father and his wife decided to kneel in prayer, and to not cease until they had obtained a clear answer as to what they could do to save their son. As the father tells the story, he and his wife were on their knees for what seemed like an eternity. They begged for an answer. None came.

Finally, as the father describes it, he and his wife came to "know" that their son would be O.K.. That was it. Nothing more. Yet, that knowledge was as real to them as a mathematical proof that two plus two equals four.

So, what did dad do the next day? And the day after that? He did the same things that he had been doing for the past months. Within less than ninety days, the son had completely abandoned the disastrous and self-destructive course that he had been on.

Skeptics might claim that all teen-agers go through a rebellious period, and that in this case, it had simply run its course. After all, nothing had really changed, had it?

Yet a different perception would suggest that something very fundamental had happened. Faith had given that mother and father a hopeful vision of the future. Faith had the power to change them. And, having changed them, the encouragement that they had been giving, the "strokes" they had been offering were no longer manipulative motivational techniques. All of a sudden, they were real and genuine and sincere. Faith changed them. And faith changed their son—for the better.

Faith, then, truly is a principle of power. As a principle of power, it is very much like any other fuel. It is burned up. It is used. It needs to be replaced.

To illustrate, let's go back to the words of Paul, faith is "... *the substance of things hoped for, the evidence of things not seen.*" With that in mind, what happens when that which is hoped for is realized? What happens when that which is not seen becomes visible?

It is by faith that I "know" that the sun will rise in the east tomorrow. By mid-morning tomorrow, that which I had previously known by faith is known by the certainty of the senses and the fact of the actual event.

The objective for all faith is exactly the same. Make it as temporary as possible! Faith that believes that a child can transcend a self-destructive approach to life needs to be coupled with as many affirmative actions as possible to make the belief a reality. Faith that I can achieve any kind of perfection must be accompanied by supportive effort.

Otherwise, it is not faith. It is merely wishful thinking.

But, faith, real faith is power. It is the power to change self. It is the power by which I can change the world—one person at a time. Starting with me.

7
Virtue

If I have the power, through faith, to start making changes, not just in myself, but in others, then it seems to follow that, all of a sudden, I have a great responsibility.

Change can be for the better, or for the worse. And if I am the cause of changing anything for the worse, then I have lost ground; I have put myself in the uncomfortable position of contributing to the corruption of the world.

This is where virtue enters the picture. Faith may be the force of life. But it is virtue that gives life a special quality, a special spirit. It is virtue that conforms thoughts and actions with the principles of morality. It is virtue that makes the practical distinctions between good and evil.

It is easy to observe that the world is more than a little confused when it comes to a common understanding of such terms as "virtue," "morality," "good," and "evil." Among the multitudes of dictionaries, I have not found two that are in complete agreement when it comes to the definitions of any of these words.

And, where there is agreement, it is often wrong. For example, one of the areas of frequent agreement as to one of the definitions of "virtue" is that it means chastity—especially on the part of a female. I am not disagreeing with the idea that chastity is an important part of virtue. It is. But, if we are agreed that God is not a respecter of persons, then we must also agree that chastity is every bit as important for a man as it is for a woman.

You already knew that. Perhaps you did not know it with

great conviction. Maybe you never really thought it out. And, perhaps, you have even lived your life in a manner completely contrary to that realization.

Nonetheless, you recognize it to be a universal and eternal truth that chastity is morally "right"—for both men and women. You believe it because you have a conscience, because you were born with a purity of heart, because that realization is a part of your spiritual being, or whatever you want to call it.

Likewise, you realize that it is "wrong" to commit murder. It is "wrong" to take that which belongs to another. And, in general terms, honesty and integrity are "good."

All of these awarenesses are part of the basic operating system that man is born with. He may ignore them, he may choose to live his life in a manner that is completely opposed to some or all of them. When he does so, he piles layer upon layer of scar tissue atop each small voice that is still saying, "this is wrong." But, he does not silence the voice. However weak it might be, it is still there.

Instinctively we know that there is more to virtue than these few things. My sense of it is that this bit of basic "pre-programming" is a divine gift and protection (for ourselves and for others) to help us get started in life without making such a muddle of things that we despair of our ability to ever get on the right track.

Plutarch, in writing about the life of Coriolanus observed, *". . . the Latin word for virtue, . . . is properly equivalent to manly courage. As if all valor and all virtue had been the same thing, they used as the common term, the name of the particular excellence."*

Plutarch was right. Courage is a strong component of virtue. Men in almost all ages have lived at a time when morality and virtue were poorly understood, if not outrightly derided. The individual who chooses to ignore the follies of the majority and to pursue a "virtuous" course is truly courageous—probably heroically so!

Another important facet of virtue, for most of us, is that we are still in the process of adding to our basic understandings of just what is—and is not—virtuous. An early pioneer commented to the effect that doing the right thing is sometimes not half so difficult as the knowing of what is the right thing to do. Living this life, facing the daily confrontations of confusions and complexities and Machiavellian twists, challenges us to continually expand our awarenesses of the moral implications of our thoughts and actions.

So far, we have discussed virtue in a context of "self." The primary beneficiaries of virtuous thought and action are ourselves. (It is also true that those whom we have not murdered, stolen from, or cheated etc. are also "beneficiaries"—although not in a positive sense).

But, there is one more step to be taken in the development of virtue within ourselves. That step is to use the faith and virtue that we have developed to foster and promote that which is good in, or for, others.

The New Testament contains several references to a remarkable phenomenon. Luke tells the story of a woman who had suffered an issue of blood for a number of years. She had spent all that she had in pursuit of a cure, but to no avail.

One day this woman came up behind Jesus in a crowd and simply touched the hem of his garment. Immediately, she was healed.

To me, the remarkable statement was, "*. . . Somebody hath touched me: for I perceive that virtue is gone out of me.*" (Luke 8:46) For a long period of time, I reflected on that verse—and several similar verses—without much real understanding. I wondered how it was possible to lose, in an apparently quantifiable sense, something that I recognized only as a characteristic of an individual. Finally, I came to understand.

I had an opportunity to render some service to a young man who, by his own actions, had placed himself in great distress with his family, with the law, and with a sizable portion of his community. To make matters worse, the young man was unwilling to accept any culpability for his predicament. My primary concern was for the welfare of his wife and infant daughter. But at the same time (and it had to be by faith—because there was no objective evidence to the contrary) I believed that this young man could turn himself around sufficiently and in time to avoid the almost certain inevitability of jail. Coupled with that faith was an intense desire that this young man would come to an honest realization of what he had done, and that it was not too late for him to make amends.

The situation was one in which the young man had attempted to assault his landlord with a baseball bat. Fortunately, the landlord was a better runner than the young man. Appropriately, the landlord pressed charges; and, inappropriately, the young man filed a countercharge claiming that it was the landlord who assaulted him with the bat. The day before the case was scheduled to go to court, the young man came to visit me in my office and asked me to intercede in his behalf—knowing that my volunteer work with street kids in the community had given me some credibility with the judge who was to hear the case.

After hearing his request, I rotated my chair so that, ostensibly, I could turn off my telephone to avoid being disturbed. More importantly, I used that moment to offer up a very short, but urgent and fervent, prayer that I might find a measure of the wisdom of Solomon as I tried to figure out how to deal with his request.

I was suddenly prompted to accept his version of what had placed him in trouble with the law. I then observed that if what he was telling me was true, then his accuser (the landlord) was a truly dangerous person who had to be held accountable for his acts—and that nothing should be done to stand in the way of justice. The matter, obviously, must continue on to court for resolution. Suddenly, the young man saw with infinite clarity that he could no longer maintain his fiction. More importantly, he no longer wanted to. The experience was personally rewarding in two ways. Obviously I was relieved and satisfied to see this young man back on a "right" path. But I also came to understand the meaning of the statement, *". . . I perceive that virtue is gone out of me."* At the moment that my young friend let go of the lie, I, too, felt virtue gone out of me. It was not a letdown, it was not the same as being "emotionally drained"—the feeling that comes after a particularly intense but unsatisfactory encounter. (By the way, the sense of loss upon "feeling virtue gone out" is not a permanent one, and the process of "re-charging" is not difficult.)

Since then, I have had the same sense of things on similar occasions. Occasionally, I have met others who have had similar experiences. I would like to believe that the having of such experiences is an indication that one has passed that portion of the test labelled "virtue." I do know, however, that having that special feeling of loss is a good indication that one is at least on the "right" path.

8
Knowledge

Knowledge is the true understanding of the character, purpose, meaning, and operation of the world and all that is in it.

If you accept this definition, then it follows that knowledge will be concerned about such things as mathematics, chemistry, medicine, physics, astronomy, language, economics, etc.—as well as those things that give character, purpose, and meaning to man himself.

Knowledge must also include the things of the Spirit. The man who is truly learning is constantly changing the boundaries between his faith and his knowledge. Education is simply the process of displacing faith by knowledge. And, with this perspective, faith becomes that which is only temporarily impenetrable by the mind and spirit of man.

This observation, extended to its logical conclusion, is that man can ultimately come to transcend faith and can come to have actual knowledge of God. That is the essence of Peter's promise—the essence of *The Second Peter Principle.*

In seeking to understand how we can obtain such knowledge, we need to discuss how it is that we, typically, obtain knowledge today. When faced with a new idea, most of us have a habit of asking, "By what authority?" For example, if it is a new idea in the field of astronomy—and if it is Carl Sagan putting forth this new idea, then most of us are accustomed to automatically accepting this new idea as proven fact.

There are at least two major problems with this approach.

First, we don't know just how it is that Carl Sagan came up with this idea. It may be that it is, in fact, the result of substantial research and that it is demonstrable and repeatable under all appropriate conditions. Or, it may be that it is simply a plausible (although totally unproved) idea advanced by a colleague of Carl Sagan. In either case, we have no objective certainty that we have added to our true understanding of anything.

The other major problem with this approach to gaining "knowledge" is that, even though we never should have started down this particular path, we are less likely to know when to stop. For example, once we have accepted Carl Sagan as an authority in the field of astronomy, it is "easy" to accept him as an authority in fields that are totally unrelated.

Such blind acceptance of an expert opinion is mental sloth. And, despite our rationalizations to the contrary, we have added only to our prejudices—not to our knowledge. There is no short-cut to knowledge.

This is where virtue enters the picture. The virtuous man has the integrity to look at all sides of an issue—to ask the more penetrating question, "Why do you say that?" Virtue will challenge our prejudices and demand that we examine the contrary evidences.

Virtue is not a respecter of persons. What is being said is more important than who is saying it. Virtue is interested in true understanding—not authoritative prejudice.

So, with all of that, the "how" of obtaining knowledge becomes self-evident. Study all sides. Weigh the evidence. Test the conclusions. Discard that which does not fit. Above all, accept the discomfort of challenging your own prejudices. By so doing, you will, at least for yourself, have proved the Apostle Paul wrong when he wrote to Timothy that in the last days that the people would be *"ever learning, and never able to come to the knowledge of the truth."*

Another way of explaining this concept is to cite an old Jewish tradition that says, in effect, *"Jews love to argue with God—*

and we have the scars to prove it!" At the risk of starting or perpetuating a stereotype, it seems to me that many Jews, in the course of their religious studies, are doing a fairly good job of teaching their children—and themselves—this "critical" kind of study, this "critical" sort of learning ("critical," not in a sense of carping, but, rather, in a sense of judicious evaluation). Volume after volume of Jewish commentaries are questioning, questioning, and considering—and questioning again.

It appears that this model of inquiry extends beyond the realm of religious study and into the everyday lives of many Jewish people. It further appears that this approach to obtaining knowledge offers a major part of the explanation as to why the Jews make—and have always made—extraordinary contributions to the arts, sciences, commerce, politics, or virtually any field of endeavor in which they have participated. Certainly, their contributions and successes have been greatly in excess of their relatively small numbers.

For these reasons, and more, it is appropriate—it is necessary—that our own quests for knowledge proceed in a similar manner. Study, and study critically, all of the disciplines that are important in your life.

Also, remember the importance of your spiritual self. Study, and study critically, the scriptures. Read some every day. Regularly. (Reading as few as five pages each day will complete both the Old and New Testaments in a year.) Then start over again. But, ponder what you read. Look for the principles. Look for experiences in your own life or in the lives around you to "test" the principles.

Let me give you a brief example. Not long ago Harold Reynolds, the professional baseball player, was in my office. He has a habit, very much like my own, of examining bookshelves to see what sorts of books are there—and what sorts of interests the owner might have.

He noted the several shelves of Judaica and old testament commentaries. We discussed, briefly, our common frustrations in reading the Old Testament—and our mutual senses of inadequacy in getting a really good understanding of a body of knowledge that we could, for the most part, only sense.

He asked me what I was working on at the moment, and I started to explain a somewhat-involved theory that had its roots in Genesis.

However, I felt prompted to not do so in a direct fashion. Rather, I asked him a series of questions about baseball and his team's performance under varying conditions. I then outlined, in very general terms, a theory that I was working on that had to do with possible physical causes of Adam's (and other's of the patriarchs) extraordinary longevity—and I then "predicted," that under one set of circumstances, his athletic performance (as well as that of his teammates) would be noticeably improved.

It turns out that the circumstances that I had anticipated had been noticed by Harold—and it was something that he had commented on to his trainers. The trainers had offered an explanation (although it was unsatisfactory because it did not fit the obvious and observable facts; and the phenomenon had remained an enigma).

But back to the subject of acquiring knowledge. I had developed a theory. I had, upon further investigation, developed incredible correlations. And, in this one instance, I had discovered *an* ability to "predict" unknown or "future" events.

I had made a step in establishing a cause and effect relationship.

Yet, more remained to be learned. I was on a right track; I had not yet acquired "knowledge."

But, I was in the process of getting a true understanding of the character, purpose, meaning, and operation of the world and *all* that is in it.

9
Temperance

One of the things which distinguishes man from the other animals is his ability to think, to reason and to govern his actions accordingly. Man is suddenly free, if he so chooses, to act other than reflexively.

As man gains knowledge, he adds to his ability to exercise restraint—to exercise temperance. Temperance, to most people today, could probably be defined as "moderation in all things."

More restrictively, the immoderate man cannot be viewed as temperate. Similarly, the individual who is a "moderate" participator in adultery, or in the drug scene, or in his hatreds, or in greed or whatever would likewise not be viewed as a temperate individual.

I do not want to conjure up visions of Carrie Nation goose-stepping down the middle of Main Street with her trusty little hatchet in hand as she advances on the nearest saloon. But, when Peter spoke of "temperance," it was in the sense of abstaining from those things which detract from the proper character, purpose, meaning and operation of one's life (which understanding comes from having gained knowledge).

Paul spoke of this process in his epistle to the Galatians:

> *This I say then, Walk in the spirit,*
> *and ye shall not fulfil the lust of the flesh.*
> *For the flesh lusteth against the*
> *Spirit, and the Spirit against the flesh:*

and these are contrary the one to the other: so that ye cannot do the things that ye would.

But if ye be led of the Spirit, ye are not under the law.

Now the works of the flesh are manifest, which are these; Adultery, fornication, uncleanness, lasciviousness,

Idolatry, witchcraft, hatred, variance, emulations, wrath, strife, seditions heresies,

Envyings, murders, drunkenness, revellings, and such like: of the which I tell you before, as I have also told you in time past, that they which do such things shall not inherit the kingdom of God.

But the fruit of the Spirit is love, joy, peace, longsuffering, gentleness, goodness, faith,

Meekness, temperance: against such there is no law.

And they that are Christ's have crucified the flesh with the affections and lusts.

If we live in the Spirit, let us also walk in the Spirit.

Galatians 5:16-25

Jacob Neusner, a professor at Brown University, makes an insightful observation, *"The will to act has to be channeled and controlled by intellect: you are what you do. Therefore, deed without deliberation is not to be taken seriously. Examination of deeds takes priority over mere repetition of what works or what feels good. For this purpose, genius is insufficient; cleverness is irrelevant. What is preferred is systematic and orderly con-*

sideration, step by step, of the principles by which one acts. The human problem . . . is not finding the motive force to do, but discovering the restraint to regulate that protean force. In the quest for restraint and self-control, the primal energies will ensure one is not bored or lacking in purpose."

Putting it all together, temperance is a major plateau in the process of perfecting self. The embryonic steps taken initially to escape the corruption of the world find a more mature and enlightened stride when one has, with diligence, taken the intervening steps of developing faith and virtue and knowledge.

The attainment of temperance in one's life is very much like receiving a college diploma; the educational process is far from complete, but a major milestone has been achieved. The educational process will continue, but with a shift in emphasis.

It is the same way in the process of perfecting self. All of the things done so far—escaping the corruption of the world, having faith, adding virtue, knowledge, and temperance—have had as their primary purpose the direct remodelling of you. The focus and interest has been intensely personal and self-centered.

The remaining steps are to strengthen what has already been accomplished, to get beyond self, and to become more concerned about others (thereby experiencing an *indirect* process of perfecting self).

10
Patience

"In your patience possess ye your souls."
Luke 21:19

In all of literature there is only one really comprehensive and archetypal model for patience. That is Job.

If you remember the story, Job was a good man. In our hierarchy of things, Job had certainly progressed through "temperance," and he effectively wrote the book when it comes to patience.

But back to the story. Job had come to the attention of Satan, and Satan accused God of having placed special protections about Job. Satan further challenged God by claiming that if Job lost all that he had, he would come, ultimately, to the point of cursing God to his face.

To make a very long and very painful story short, Satan made life miserable for Job. Job lost all that he had—and he was an extremely wealthy man to begin with. He lost his family. He lost his health. His friends turned on him.

Yet, through the entire ordeal, Job maintained his perspective. He endured. Here is a sampling of some of his comments during the times of his trial:

> *"What? shall we receive good at the hand of God, and shall we not receive evil?*
>
> *"For I know that my redeemer liveth, and that he shall stand at the latter day upon*

the earth: And though after my skin worms destroy this body, yet in my flesh shall I see God:

"*. . . when he hath tried me, I shall come forth as gold.*

"*. . . Behold, the fear of the Lord, that is wisdom; and to depart from evil is understanding.*"

There is no reason to believe it was any easier for Job to have achieved his level of personal perfection than it is for us. If God truly is the same yesterday as he is today, then Job will have had as much of a struggle with self as we are having today. And, just as surely as Job had to face his challenges, we will have to face ours.

The important thing to remember is that bad things happen. Irrespective of their magnitude and frequency, they do not change one thing about the "rightness" of escaping the corruption of the world. They do not change one thing about the nature of faith. They do not change one thing about the enduring value of virtue. They do not change by one cent the priceless value of real knowledge. They do not—cannot—replace temperance. But they hurt. They have the power to distract—if we let them.

That is the whole point. We need to be tried. We need to strengthen the base that we have already built so that it becomes second nature to us.

We need to maintain the perspective of Job and realize, as did he, that when all of this is said and done, "*. . . when he hath tried me, I shall come forth as gold.*"

11
Godliness

Of all of the terms in Peter's progression, "godliness" is the one that seems to be the most difficult to understand—not only in terms of meaning, but also in terms of placement.

One common understanding of "godliness" would have it be the quality or state of being devoutly conforming to the word of God. Yet, that definition does not really fit within the context of the verses given in the first chapter of Second Peter. The understanding of those verses suggests that if one does all of the listed things, *then,* one will have become "godly" in the common sense of understanding.

A search of New Testament scriptures in an attempt to know how the term was used at the time of Peter provides the desired understanding. For instance, Paul, in his two epistles to Timothy makes several comments. In First Timothy he says, *"But refuse profane and old wives fables, and exercise thyself rather unto godliness."* (I Timothy 4:7). And in his next epistle, he writes, *"Of these things put them in remembrance, charging them before the Lord that they strive not about words to no profit, but to the subverting of the hearers. Study to show thyself approved unto God, a workman that needeth not to be ashamed, rightly dividing the word of truth. But shun profane and vain babblings: for they will increase unto more ungodliness."* (II Timothy 2:14-16).

In the first sense, Paul is defining *un*godliness as treating things with abuse and contempt and being caught up in things that are not true. In the second sense, he is again defining *un*godliness—

and this time adding the notion that it includes argumentativeness.

With all of this it is tempting to look for a one-word synonym. "Respect" or "consideration" come close to fitting; but there needs to be added a sense of calmness and certainty that comes from a good understanding of the true principles involved in whatever situation is at hand. It maintains a "respect" for the free agency of others. It is "considerate" of honest attempts to understand. And this brings us almost back to our first definition which would be much more accurate if it were to suggest a *willingness* to conform to this growing understanding of the spirit of the law—of the spirit of God. (Remembering, of course that it is not yet the *doing*—it is simply establishing the appropriate framework and approach where the actual *doing* becomes possible.)

This new-found understanding avoids the strident contentions that are a too-frequent part of discussions of our most vital issues.

In a family setting, I can give you a personal example. My son and I used to go around and around, getting nowhere except mutually hot under the collar. In the course of our "discussions," he was often prone to say, "In my opinion, . . . ".

Such a statement would usually set my teeth on edge. From my perspective, I had experience, years of study, and exquisitely logical and well-presented cases that even the village idiot could comprehend in a flash. (I was humble, too!)

Against this formidable array of the wisdom of the world, my son wanted his "opinion," his unreasoned and inexperienced "guess" to carry equal weight in the arena of truth and knowledge. There are those who would say that we didn't "communicate." They would have been right.

And then, one day I finally "let go." I don't know if it was wisdom—or exhaustion. I finally acknowledged that my son truly did have his own free agency. He had the gift of a fine mind. But, the choice of using it—or not using it—was uniquely his.

With that realization on my part, things changed. More precisely, I changed. I came to more easily "accept" his opinions. Our discussions were no longer arenas in which the strengths of wills were tested. Rather, they became forums in which ideas were given a full range of play. I had finally learned how to set the stage for fruitful discussions where real enlightenment might be found.

In a broader setting, another example of this kind of "ungodliness" can be found in the popular radio and television talk or panel shows where, in a sense of "fairness," opposing sides of a common issue are "discussed" simultaneously. Too typically, a panel member on each side will apparently proceed from the assumption that the louder and more strident his "rational" presentation, the more likely that he will win converts to his position. In the rating books, it may be "good" radio or television. But that is all that can be claimed. Whatever truths might have been put forth are simply lost in strident sanctimony.

With this newly found and "respectful" sense of things, the placement of "godliness" after "patience" and before "brotherly kindness" makes perfect sense. Once a person has improved himself up to and through the point of temperance, and once a person has had those improvements refined, tested, and purified by the trials of patience and endurance—once all of this has happened, that person has gained, not only the strengths, but also the credibility to be of material assistance to his neighbor.

Obviously, the next step is to deal with one's neighbor—to deal with all men with an appropriately respectful and considerate attitude, an appropriate frame of mind.

That appropriate approach is what Peter calls godliness.

12
Brotherly Kindness

When Peter speaks of brotherly kindness there is little doubt that he will be misunderstood. Kindness may not be all that frequently encountered today, but that does not detract from our awareness that kindness embodies a sense of genuine helpfulness, a genuine concern for another's welfare. It also includes sympathy and understanding—a willingness to forgive. And it includes one more essential element. It requires actually doing something or a series of somethings for another.

Some years ago I received a telephone call from an acquaintance who lives in another part of the country. In the course of her telephone call, she proudly proclaimed that she had telephoned a dial-a-prayer service in my behalf, and that those people were now praying for my well-being. I was pleased that she had achieved enough of a measure of faith to even be concerned about the efficacy of prayer. But, I was worried that she had confused this simple act with the notion that she had really *done* something. I was prompted to relate to her an observation made by C. S. Lewis when he said, *"It is easy to pray for a boor; it is difficult to go and visit one."*

I am not telling this little story to imply that I am a boor (although at times the title may fit). Rather, the point that Lewis is making is that we may have warm, cuddly, kind feelings in behalf of another person. We may even—and in fact, ought to—offer up fervent prayers in his or her behalf. But unless we actually bestir ourselves to action, unless we actually use the talents that we have been given, unless we start putting to practical use the improvements that we have been making in ourselves—unless we start doing all of this, then we have totally missed the point. The exhortation to add brotherly kindness is a call to action!

13
Charity

I thought that I knew what charity meant until I went to the dictionary to assure myself that my understanding was the common one. Again, I found that there are nearly as many definitions as there are dictionaries. However, the *Oxford English Dictionary* has earned its reputation as *the* definitive dictionary of the English language. In addressing "charity," it directs the readers attention to the thirteenth chapter of First Corinthians:

> *Though I speak with the tongues of men*
> *and angels, and have not charity, I am become*
> *as sounding brass, or a tinkling cymbal.*
> *And though I have the gift of prophecy,*
> *and understanding all mysteries, and all knowledge;*
> *and though I have all faith, so that I could remove*
> *mountains, and have not charity, I am nothing.*
> *And though I bestow all my goods to feed the*
> *poor, and though I give my body to be burned,*
> *and have not charity, it profiteth me nothing.*
> *Charity suffereth long, and is kind;*
> *charity envieth not; charity vaunteth not*
> *itself, is not puffed up,*
> *Doth not behave itself unseemly, seeketh*
> *not her own, is not easily provoked,*
> *thinketh no evil;*

Rejoiceth not in iniquity, but rejoiceth
in the truth;
Beareth all things, believeth all things,
hopeth all things, endureth all things.
Charity never faileth: but whether there
be prophecies, they shall fail; whether
there shall be tongues, they shall cease;
whether there shall be knowledge,
it shall vanish away.
For we know in part, and we prophesy
in part.
But when that which is perfect is
come, then that which is in part shall
be done away.
When I was a child, I spake as a child,
I understood as a child, I thought as a
child: but when I became a man, I put away
childish things.
For now we see through a glass, darkly;
but then face to face: now I know in part;
but then I shall know even as also I am known.
And now abideth faith, hope, charity,
these three; but the greatest of these
is charity.

I Corinthians 13:1-13

These verses give a sense of the value of charity. They also give several characteristics of that virtue. But, they leave me wanting just a bit more.

The traditional Christian definition of the word would have it to be "love," or more often, the pure love of Christ.

Again, we are faced with the question, "What, exactly, does that mean?" What is "the pure love of Christ"?

More precisely, what is love? M. Scott Peck, Jr. in his book *The Road Less Traveled,* offers the simplest definition when he suggests that love is personal sacrifice in favor of another's spiritual growth.

Another definition of charity provides for kindness or help for the needy or the suffering.

With these two definitions in mind, it is now possible to put them together and to begin to comprehend "charity."

"Charity" is a pure and refined love that makes sacrifices for the needy and for the suffering.

With a wisdom born of the pain and effort of personal development, it recognizes that almost all of us are needy and suffering in one or more ways. "Charity" recognizes that the neediest and the most suffering are probably the least "lovable" among us—and it is "charity" that loves them all the more. It is a love that exists, not in spite of their needs and weaknesses, but *because* of them.

"Charity" is emotional and spiritual maturity. The addition of charity, like the addition of temperance, is a quantum leap in ones's personal growth. When an individual reaches this stage of his development, when an individual sets out to more perfectly love others—to make sacrifices in favor of their spiritual growth—he does so with an awesome sense of the enormous responsibility and the divine nature of the opportunity that he is taking upon himself.

In so doing, *every* characteristic, trait and virtue discussed up to this point finds its maturation, its fullness, its perfection. This is charity.

14
How Am I Doing?

So far we have discussed, in a very basic way, the main elements of Peter's formula for perfection. When I initially achieved this level of understanding for myself, I felt the simultaneous tugs of both encouragement and frustration.

I was heartened by the fact that I now understood the relationships. And I felt enthused because I had a clearer sense of just what was intended when the various terms were being used. Further, because the whole of it was strengthened and reinforced by the scrutiny that I had applied, I was more convinced than ever of the ultimate soundness of the formula and of the truthfulness of the promise.

The discouragement came, however, in trying to apply it to my own life. I continued to be plagued by an inability to determine exactly where I was on the continuum, and by an inability to know what it was I needed to be working on next.

For example, in some areas of my life, I could honestly lay claim to having had the patience of Job. But in other areas, I was still struggling with escaping the corruption of the world. To further confuse the issue, in still other areas, I thought I could give myself a "B+" or maybe even an "A" in brotherly kindness.

But the basic question remained. How am I doing?

Finally, understanding came. I had been attempting to solve a two-dimensional problem with a one-dimensional approach.

Actually, there was something of an evolutionary process—even in this realization.

First, I realized that this being called "me" is really very complex. I have responsibilities as an individual, as a husband, as a father, etc.. And as I reflect upon how "I" respond to different stimuli, I can see quite clearly that my responses are not consistent. I was not saying that this was the way that things should be; but it was a true assessment of how things actually were with "me." And that started the understanding of why I was having such a difficult time of developing a satisfactory assessment of where "I" was. There were multiple "I"s!

That realization was the final evolutionary step of my discovering a practical approach to the *Second Peter Principle.* If I could identify all of the major roles that I fulfill in this life, then, with great precision, I could start applying the yardstick of the *Second Peter Principle* to my own life. I could start answering, with precision, such questions as, "How is your patience—as a parent (and, more precisely still, as a parent of teenagers)?" I might not like the answer, but without any reservations or qualifications, I could answer the question.

It now remained only for me to identify the major roles in my life.

15
Roles

Physical and Mental

The most fundamental role is that of keeping the physical and mental me going. Without that, there are no other roles to be fulfilled. The New Testament puts forth as an important idea, a commandment really, that we need to love ourselves before we love others. Stated another way, we cannot care for others until we first learn to care for ourselves. Further, we cannot have an honest love for ourselves unless and until there is something there that is lovable.

We need to put forth the effort to make it a reality. We need to be clean. We need to have a physical vitality that energizes all that we do. We need to be mentally alive and alert. We need to feed our minds and our souls with good literature, good art, good associations—those things that inspire and urge us to greater heights and that light our way.

We need these things for "us." They are the means to an even greater end. They can provide a model for the rest of our roles.

Spouse

Being a spouse is a unique responsibility. It is a role that I can solemnify with divine authority. I may choose to enter such a relationship solely under the auspices of the civil authorities; but, even then, it is a relationship recognized by God—and, therefore, I am accountable before Him for my marital behavior. Being a spouse is a distinct role, and my attitudes and actions must treat it as such.

Parent

For some, being a parent is an unplanned and incidental adjunct to being a spouse. Regardless, it is not a role that can properly be delegated. I have learned also that it is a role that is not terminated.

My children are now grown; my daughters are married with children of their own. Conventional wisdom would have it that my active role as a parent is finished, but I have learned—and am continuing to learn—that the role is not over.

The arena has changed. The concerns remain the same. The means of dealing with them has been changed. I am still a parent.

Temporal Stewardship

I have a temporal stewardship. The things that I work at in this world are my responsibility. I give my work effort and skill in exchange for those things that I both need and want. (This definition includes school, for my younger friends.) As a temporal steward, I have unique associations, responsibilities and authorities.

Spiritual Stewardship

My list of roles also includes that of a spiritual stewardship. Early on, we discussed the notion that there is a spiritual component to man. That component likewise needs to be nurtured, to grow, and to mature. It does that, primarily, through service to others.

It is also my belief that, as we wend our way through each step of *The Second Peter Principle,* we need encouragement and support. Religious institutions *should* provide this support. If they do, it is because they recognize these principles; and they provide opportunities for such service. They should also provide guidance and encouragement; and they should ask for accountability.

Such service is simply a model for what is ultimately intended to become as second nature in the individual.

Spiritual stewardship also includes those things that prepare, strengthen, enlighten, and inspire the spirit—things such as scripture study and prayer as well as service to, and support of, the religious institution to which you belong.

Neighbor

All of us are also neighbors. We live in a community of men. It is often a community that is under-funded and under-staffed. It is frequently contentious.

Nonetheless, it asks our help—in the PTA, the fire department, sometimes even in a political party. But always, as a "good Samaritan."

Enemy (Passive)

Finally, all of us are, at one time or another, an enemy. Even though I would not choose to be the enemy of any man, I cannot always control how it is that other men might view me.

Those individuals who incorporate *The Second Peter Principle* in their lives will develop strong convictions. People who develop strong convictions will have them tested.

That testing process can be painful—and not just for the individual with the convictions. Those who seek to tear down what you have been working so diligently to build, because of their failures, may come to view you as an enemy.

This is often the most difficult role of all. When someone is really intent upon doing harm to you or to someone close to you, it can be difficult to conquer the desire to "get even."

But, try as I might, I do not find any exceptions in the writings of Peter—or in the teachings of Christ. I am still commanded to show forth patience, godliness, brotherly kindness, even charity. Especially charity. Even to my enemies.

So, at times, I am an enemy—hopefully, only in a passive sense.

Child

As I currently perceive things, this is a role to which we do not usually give conscious thought until after the point in time that we have achieved our own measures of independence. Even then, any really profound considerations of our relationships to our parents (our roles as children) are usually deferred until such time as we, ourselves, become parents.

Being a child is almost as new and difficult an experience as being a parent. Training for both roles is, in the final analysis, "on the job." We make more mistakes than we would like. Hopefully, we learn from them.

Also hopefully, we gain a greater empathy for our own parents. What was so easy to be critical of yesterday now becomes more easily understood as we struggle with our own weaknesses, foibles, and failures.

With this new-found insight, it can be quite enlightening to review our relationships with our own parents—and to do so within the context of the steps of *The Second Peter Principle.*

I do not see this as something that plagues us day after day. I do see it as something that is very worthwhile to go through once, or even once per parent.

Although I am not prepared to be dogmatic about this, nor to try to teach it as an eternal truth, I nonetheless believe that so doing will fulfill the spirit of the commandment, *"Honor thy mother and thy father: that thy days may be long upon the land . . . .*"

16
The Second Peter Prescription

Several years ago I put together a little matrix that contained the elements of the *Second Peter Principle* across the top and a listing of the various roles that I have down the left side. With apologies to Dr. Peter, I have called this little card the Second Peter Prescription. The checked off boxes to the left represent the growth that I have already achieved; the un-checked boxes to the right are my personal prescription for "moral perfection"—for wholeness.

The Second Peter Prescription

Roles	Escape Corruption	Have Faith	Add Virtue	Add Knowledge	Add Temperance	Add Patience	Add Godliness	Add Brotherly Kindness	Add Charity
Physical/Mental									
Spouse									
Parent									
Temporal Steward									
Spiritual Steward									
Neighbor									
Enemy (Passive)									

". . . that by these ye might be partakers of the divine nature . . ."

I put the Prescription together with two seemingly simple and straightforward purposes in mind.

First, by considering the virtues in relation to each of the roles, I expected that I would be able to more accurately identify my strengths and my weaknesses. I also expected that I would be able to begin to function with a great deal more efficiency. Recognizing that each of the virtues must be added in a specific sequence, I would avoid dissipating my energies in the premature pursuit of a particular virtue.

Looking back, I remember that I had one more expectation as well. I thought the process would be simple. And easy. It was neither. However, the use of the matrix did fulfill the two basic objectives—defining where I was, and identifying what I needed to work on next.

My first realization was that, while I had developed a good understanding of the definitions of each of the virtues, I was not yet finished with the basic task of getting the terms defined. For example, it was easy to be satisfied with my earlier understanding of "escaping the corruption of the world." But, I now had to ask, "What, exactly, does that mean as a spouse? Or as a parent?"

There were occasions where it seemed as if I was spending weeks understanding the meaning of a specific virtue in a given role—and then only days in its actual accomplishment.

My initial reaction to this experience was to think that there was a fundamental flaw in the approach. That feeling was strengthened as I encountered more instances of the same. Often, the specific definition was more difficult than the defined task.

Finally, understanding came. The process was not flawed. The definitions that were coming so slowly—and that seemed to be impeding progress—were actually a part of the process itself. The definitions were, in some cases, penetrating insights into the principles that govern—me in particular, and man in general.

My assumptions about dissipating energy by working on certain virtues prematurely have also been modified. A number of times in the last several years, I have faced situations that have seemed to be so desperate, so "unsolvable" that only charity with all of its attendant perfections could rise to the needs of the situation. On the basis of my initial assumption, it would be inappropriate to even make the effort; without the proper foundation, the effort would seem doomed to failure.

I have learned that the assumption is wrong. More important, I have learned much about the process of growth. In those instances where we are in a unique position to bring peace or comfort or to render some essential assistance that demands greater purity, perfection, or patience than we currently possess, we can, and should, enter into the fray. Diligently. With humility. And with a trepidation born of a recognition of the risks—and of the responsibilities. There is a divine dispensation, in such instances, that permits us to tap unknown reservoirs of strength and ability, to achieve in needed moments when only charity will really do.

The next day, when the demands of the moment have passed, the task at hand is back to the perfecting of virtue or knowledge or whatever you were working on before the crisis arose. Certainly, because of the experience, you have grown. You are better prepared for the next crisis. Your faith has been strengthened. The path has been better illuminated.

And you are still faced with the task of making each of the virtues into an automatic response, a true second-nature.

By the time that I had come to these realizations, I was delighted. Experience was beginning to prove the validity and workability of the concept. True, the realization was taking a slightly different form than I had originally anticipated. But, somehow, the differences seemed to make the whole of it stronger and more valuable.

The word that came to my mind was serendipity. Unexpected benefits. The last several years have seen a number of additional applications of the matrix. Each new application has brought with it pleasantly surprising benefits—benefits in the form of improved relations or quicker solutions or closer friendships or more profound teaching moments—and sometimes all of these simultaneously.

One example occurred at work. It was time to give employees periodic evaluations. Using the Second Peter Prescription, I had just completed an initial assessment of myself. I had mixed feelings about the appropriateness of using the prescription (recognizing that how an employee is doing as a spouse or as a parent is, essentially, none of my business as an employer). Nonetheless, I decided to go forward with the approach. I began the reviews with an explanation of the prescription, and I invited the employee to review me and my performance—using the Second Peter Prescription as a guide. Following that, I gave the employee another blank sheet; and I asked him to then evaluate himself.

The results were consistent, and, while I don't remember precisely what I initially expected from the exercise, I can say that my expectations were dramatically exceeded.

First, the evaluations of me were remarkably "on target." There was candor in identifying my shortcomings. There was generally an awareness of what changes I was currently attempting to incorporate into my life. There was also something of a tendency to give me better marks in a given area than I had given myself (and, in this, I detected no tendency to "butter up" the boss).

When it came to the employees' self-evaluations, these tended to be more critical than I would have been. Much thought and reflection was given by each individual as he considered himself in a number of new lights.

Since then I have observed two major—and apparent long term—benefits accruing from the approach. First, the employee recognized in me a concern that went beyond him solely as a potential profit center. The concerns were for the "whole" individual. That was recognized, and it was appreciated.

Second, the use of the prescription seemed to foster a measure of introspection—an ongoing process of self-evaluation that was infinitely more productive than my periodic reviews.

Closer to home, I have from time to time observed friends

and neighbors struggling with a particular problem of one sort or another. As I contemplated their various situations, I found myself taking what I knew of them and mentally filling out a Second Peter Prescription. It seemed, more often than not, that the solution to their particular quandary was then readily apparent to me. I had long since learned, however, that one of the more effective ways of diminishing your base of friends is to always know exactly what it is that someone else should do.

My experiences at the office, however, had taught me how relatively easy it is to talk about the Second Peter Prescription. I started doing so.

I quickly learned that it was no longer necessary to "tell" others the solutions to their problems. Simply show them the principles contained in the Second Peter Prescription and they will find the solutions for themselves. Better still, you will not have jeopardized a friendship. You will have strengthened it.

At about this time, I discovered something else that I could attribute to the Second Peter Prescription—at least as an indirect benefit. Once you have discussed the principles and the prescription with someone, there is usually a subtle change in the relationship. Prior to my having stumbled onto all of this, I would have described myself as a very private and introverted person. It was not my habit to discuss things of a very personal nature, and especially not those things that I viewed as weaknesses.

Discussing the Second Peter Prescription has a way of dropping those barriers. It does so in a non-threatening manner. The result is that all associations touched by the principle and the prescription become more meaningful.

As time progressed, I discovered that there was one area of the Second Peter Prescription that appeared to be static. I considered myself fortunate to not have any active enemies at the time—but in their absence, my performance in this area would remain speculative. However, I have discovered that there is at least one thing that I can do in anticipation of the time when I shall have to respond to an enemy. I can add to my knowledge.

I have come to realize that evil is not just an abstraction. There are individuals who set out, consciously, to do harm to others. To be able to show forth patience, kindness—even charity—to such individuals taxes the limits of my imagination. Yet, faith tells me that if I gain sufficient knowledge about the true character and destitution of evil, and if I have diligently progressed in all of the other areas of my life, then I shall be able to meet even this challenge.

One last set of general comments about the Second Peter Prescription might help put most of the preceding comments into perspective.

My experience has been such that patience appears to be my greatest challenge to date. That which was as solid as a bedrock of granite yesterday appears, today, to be floating precariously on a sea of quicksand. Compared to my troubles, Job never had it so good. Worse, when the limits of patience are being tried in one area, there is so much misery that it spills over into neighboring roles as well.

Aside from a little exaggeration, is there something of a familiar ring in that description? Isn't it the case that when the high water marks hit our lives, we are beset by doubts and uncertainties, and maybe even a certain element of fear? Do we start to question our abilities to think, and even the basic premises upon which we have built our lives?

This was the experience of Job. By choosing the Second Peter Principle and Prescription, it is an experience that we choose for ourselves. Hopefully, none of us will experience it to the same extent as Job. But, it will be a trial.

Drawing upon my own experience again, I can say only that when the creek rises, the Second Peter Prescription serves as a very effective life-line. Somehow, in the midst of the chaos of the mind during trying times, a simple review of the prescription will be all that it takes to restore perspective and peace of mind.

Having observed this phenomenon, this calming effect, I have sought for an understanding of why this should be. The card is not a talisman nor an amulet of any sort. It contains no "magical" properties.

Yet it comes close to containing a synthesis of the gospel message. An act as simple as a review of one's progress on such a divine scale may, somehow, serve as a recommitment, as the renewing of a covenant. It may be that the application of the prescription simply "taps in" to the eternal principles that glue the prescription together, and thereby restores order and sanity to life.

In the last analysis, however, I simply do not know why the prescription works in this fashion. Nor do I know why it has such a salutary effect on friends and neighbors and employees. Perhaps it is sufficient to recognize that it simply does have these effects.

Lastly, I would comment that the real value of the card is to serve as a constant reminder—a reminder of who you already are—a reminder of where you are headed.

* * *

When you tear out the sheet of cards from the inside jacket of this book, you will discover that you have four copies the card.

Seemingly, you will need only one.

However, the other three cards are just as important. They are intended for your use as you teach others about *The Second Peter Principle* and the Second Peter Prescription. As you teach, give the cards away.

It is important that you do teach. It is important to your friends. It is equally important to you. As you teach, you will come to better understand the principles yourself.

While we are on the subject of physical reminders, I would tell you of one other thing that I do. And for this I also give thanks to Ben Franklin, who did something similar, but without the conveniences provided by today's technology.

Each day I review my Second Peter Prescription card and carefully consider just what it is that I can do today in each of the roles that I am working on. I then note these "action items" on a small "post it" note and attach this small slip of paper to my daily calendar. Since this little piece of paper covers most of the space allocated for the day's appointments, I cannot survive the day without being frequently reminded that I have important work and commitments that go beyond the more temporal considerations.

17
A Case History

In an attempt to illustrate some of the power of The Second Peter Prescription, and of the principles involved, I would like to relate a personal experience. All told, the time covered is a bit over a year. In looking back, I can see how it helped me to grow through a difficult time. More importantly, it literally established the perspectives that saved a life!

Several years ago, I was serving as a Guardian Ad Litum in the juvenile court system. By way of explanation, in Washington state, where I live, the Department of Social and Health Services (DSHS) is charged, by law, with the task of putting dysfunctional or troubled families back together. However, the court system recognizes that this may not always be in the best interests of a child—particularly in those cases where there has been physical or sexual abuse or where the parent is patently and profoundly incapable of caring for the child. Hence, a Guardian Ad Litum who is a specially trained volunteer, may be appointed by the court.

At that time, I had only recently discovered The Second Peter Prescription, and, by my own grading, I was working on "temperance" as a "neighbor." I certainly could not have given myself any kind of passing grade for "patience" in this category. I was an outspoken critic of the juvenile court system, suggesting frequently that the actions mandated were usually too little, too late—if not just plain misguided.

In any case, the system was badly over-burdened and understaffed, which is probably why my "contrarianism" was tolerated.

This was my state of development when I was asked to take a case involving a young mother (late twenties) and her two children who had been removed from the home and placed in foster care.

The mother was described to me as alcoholic, drug dependent, possibly suicidal, and in a "living together arrangement" with an individual who was alcoholic, drug dependent, and physically abusive. The home was described as so filthy as to represent a health hazard; the children (ages eight and six) were exhibiting disturbing behavioral problems—and they had been placed in counselling. The only thing really surprising about the report was the indication that DSHS was moving aggressively to terminate parental rights in this case. My experience up to that point in time had been that DSHS, even in those cases most obviously dictating termination of parental rights, would not take action until virtually forced to by the concerted actions of the Guardian, the Attorney General, and the presiding judge.

With all of that as background, I began to call upon those involved as part of my own investigation. I visited the children in their foster home. That visit was a wonderful surprise. Usually, a foster home is unworkable over any protracted period because the dysfunctionality of the first home is largely transferred to the foster home. In this case, however, the foster parents were so mature and so loving as to transcend the usual impossibilities of such a situation.

My next visit was to the mother. When she answered the door I was immediately struck by her countenance and her surroundings. Her hair was uncombed, her cheeks were wet and stained from fresh tears and the blurring of yesterday's make-up. It was two in the afternoon, and although I had an appointment to meet her at that time, she had not yet dressed for the day; a soiled robe covered her night-clothes. Her home was in almost complete chaos. Kitchen and dishes had not seen soap nor water for at least ten days, and the odor suggested that trash had not been removed for at least as long.

Such scenes are not uncommon to those who spend any time

working with troubled and neglected youth. But, what was different in this situation was that *no* attempt at any measure of cleaning was discernible. Dysfunctional parents will usually put forth some effort to "prove" to the social workers or the guardian, or whoever that, "see, it isn't really like they said."

Not this time. There was no effort to impress nor to deceive.

One look at that mother was enough to put real flesh and meaning to the earlier, largely speculative report, that "there may be some suicidal tendencies on the part of the mom." This was a woman who had lost her children temporarily. This was a woman who believed that she would lose them permanently. This was a woman who was a slave to her addictions, and who was disgusted with the debased life that she was living to satisfy them.

This was a mother who desperately loved her children, but one who could not care for herself. Her sense of failure was nearly absolute.

She had no friends, no supportive relatives. All she really had was an abusive, live-in boyfriend upon whom she depended for drugs and alcohol.

She had no hope. The concern about suicide was no longer speculative. It was real and immediate.

As I surveyed this situation, my own mind was caught up in the turmoil of the moment. My concerns were supposed to be for the welfare of the children; DSHS was supposed to be concerned for the welfare of the mother. However, I was already well aware that the DSHS caseworker had absolutely no sympathy for the mother. More precisely, there was an obvious animosity. Worse yet, I found myself being caught up in the infectiousness of the hopelessness of the situation.

At this moment, *The Second Peter Principle*/Prescription came to mind. I had not been using it for long at this point, and I was still discovering pieces of its potential. But, the major lesson that I had already learned was that its greatest power was in the discipline of forming an adequate foundation. From a personal perspective in this particular situation, I instantly knew exactly where I was. I needed to find some measure of faith, some measure of hope before I could do anything of any value for the mother.

On the surface of it, I was asking for the impossible. Yet . . .

It was one of those moments that knows no solution other than to offer up a brief, silent and desperately fervent prayer asking for guidance, asking for a vision of the good—or at least for the good that might potentially be.

That brief prayer was rewarded, not with guidance, and not with any kind of improved vision. But, there did come a profound sense that it was simply going to be OK.

I found myself telling the mother, "It's going to be OK. You are going to get your children back."

The mother smiled, briefly, through her tears—and, for a moment at least, she believed.

I also tried to offer a few words of additional encouragement to the mother, and we set an appointment to continue the interview in one week's time.

I left the house more than a little amazed at my promise to the mother. First of all, I had no authority to make such a commitment, and secondly, even if I had that authority, common sense would have prevented an immediate return of the children.

Anyway, it was time to find out much more about the situation. I drove to the DSHS caseworker's office, and I expressed my concerns to her about what I perceived as a real potential for suicide. The caseworker noted my concern. She then expressed her opinion as to the manipulative nature of the mother, and I was advised to not worry about it. I then borrowed the caseworker's file and sat down in an adjacent cubicle to learn what I could. At the end of a half hour's review, I knew little more than I had earlier—except that the caseworker had identified the children's maternal grandmother. Although the caseworker had voiced some initial optimism that the grandmother might help, subsequent investigations had ruled her out as having any current capacity for familial assistance. The last known whereabouts of the children's father was the state prison in a neighboring state. No help.

One week later, I again visited the mother. There was little change in the home. But, this time the mother was dressed. Her hair, still damp, had just been washed. Her face was clean. And she was hurting. She said, simply, "I'm sick." She had had no alcohol or drugs for just over twenty-four hours. She was suffering the pains of withdrawal.

We sat down to continue the interview started a week earlier. I began by telling her a story.

The story was about a young girl who at the age of fourteen joined the Mormon Church with her sixteen-year-old sister and her mother—along with, and basically at the instigation of, her step-father. The girl enjoyed the associations with the church and its emphasis on strong family values. Yet, within less than two years, she had been raped by her step-father. Her sister had, likewise, been the object of his incests.

The girl ran away from home, from school, from everything that had ever been positive in her life. She went into a downward spiral—accelerated by drugs and alcohol. She married a man who, because of his own drug dealings and drug-induced assaults, was given a substantial prison sentence. Two children were the only positive thing from this short and disastrous union. The downward spiral continued, and progressed from one abusive relationship to another.

Reporting on the current status of the family, I indicated that the step-father had been excommunicated from the Mormon Church because of his incest.

At this point, the dam broke. The mother began to sob, and then to cry. It was like nothing that I had ever before seen. It was almost as if I were not there. The tears came in a literal torrent.

It is axiomatic that no man really knows what to do in the presence of a woman's tears. The welling-up of even a small tear because of a small hurt or grief is, for me, difficult to deal with.

This was not a small hurt; and I could do nothing but sit, wait, and wish for greater talents of consolation.

Finally, recovering some of her composure, the mother said, *"This is the first time in thirteen years that I have had any sense that there might be some justice in this life for me."* The tears came again. But this time the anguish was gone, the remaining tears were simply rinsing away some unseen residue.

It would be nice to be able to report that this one dramatic moment was the instant cure. It was not. But, it was a beginning. It was a small demonstration that at least one person knew—and perhaps understood—a bit of it.

The one-day start toward sobriety did not survive even another day. Escaping the corruption of the world, or even just pieces of it can be overwhelming for some.

Yet, this mother was less concerned with escaping the corruption of the world than she was with the issue of virtue. She could not accept the notion that as a child, as the victim of an incestuous rape, that she had done nothing wrong—that her real innocence had not been touched. And then, the memories of subsequent—and current events would come to her mind. For her, virtue, so highly prized and desired, was something stolen from her and then later flung away. She had little hope for her future.

I asked a few questions, and I found out who her Mormon bishop was. I telephoned him, explained my position and my concerns, and asked if he might be of assistance. He voiced an eager willingness to try.

Several days later, the mother, the bishop, and I met for lunch. The mother, hesitantly, described her history and current situation to him. In response, he quickly outlined some of the temporal assistance that could be provided through his offices (he was a medical doctor) and in his capacity as a bishop.

What impressed me most, however, was his quick discernment of her mental and spiritual state. In quoting Isaiah, he promised her, "*. . . though your sins be as scarlet, they shall be as white as snow. . . .* " With that promise, she seemed to brighten a bit, seemed to almost believe.

I left them, somewhat convinced—certainly more hopeful—that this mother had now found a support system that could strengthen her to the point where my earlier promise could be realized.

Unfortunately, despite the efforts of her bishop, she could not, or would not do her part in following up with her commitments—either to the bishop or to the juvenile court.

Review after review, hearing after hearing saw no real progress—except in the passage of time toward that minimum point after which the DSHS caseworker could petition the court to permanently terminate her parental rights.

During this period, I would check in on her from time to time, and bring her home with me on occasion for a hot meal and for an opportunity to just sit and talk.

It was on one of these occasions that I outlined *The Second Peter Principle* and Prescription to her. I suggested, hopefully respectfully, that her concerns for virtue were "putting the cart before the horse." She simply had to walk away from her addictions and the living together associations that were feeding them. I further suggested that, in her case, the doing of those two things would also be a magnificent act of faith—and that she would grow quickly from that point forward.

She nodded politely, humoring me, I guess. She thanked my wife for a good meal, and she went home.

It was at about this time that the children's father's location and current circumstances became known. He was out of prison and gainfully employed, and he wanted his children.

At the time, I was travelling extensively with my business. I took the occasion of one of those trips to make a small detour to visit the father. Clearly, he had made great strides in turning his life around. He was to be saluted for his own personal successes. My only concerns as a Guardian Ad Litum was the live-in relationship that he had with his girlfriend—the kids had already seen way too much of that.

Several weeks later, the girlfriend had moved out, and the

court gave him temporary custody of the children. Everybody expected that it would become permanent within a few months.

Being something of an incurable romantic and believing in happy endings, I did my share of speculating that maybe mom and dad would get back together—and that this would be the way that my earlier, rash promise could be fulfilled.

In fact, several weeks after that, the mother did leave the state. She moved so that she could be close to her children. The few subsequent reports that I did hear from DSHS quickly ended any fantasies about the mom and dad getting back together. Because of transferred jurisdictions, I then assumed that I would never hear, as Paul Harvey says, *"the rest of the story."* I was wrong.

About a week before Christmas, late in the evening, I received a telephone call. The connection was poor, and the voice was weak and trembling, *"Brother Hamilton, this is _____ (the mother). I had to call you and tell you that, as of this minute, I have been dry for thirty days. I have not had anything to drink or any drugs at all for the last month. And guess what?"*

I couldn't begin to guess.

She said, *"I've got a job. I'm a part-time custodian. Guess where?"* Not pausing to give me a chance to make a guess she continued, *"I looked up my bishop here. He is a wonderful man. He is meeting with me once a week. The missionaries are teaching me about the church, and I am working at the church as a custodian. And, I have a roommate.* She *is a big help and support."* (I couldn't miss the emphasis put on the word "she" when she spoke of her roommate—her way of telling me that her past living-together arrangements were truly a thing of the past.

Further, the children were doing well. She saw them frequently. With an audible smile in her voice she explained that they were turning out to be more of a handful and a responsibility than the father had anticipated. She was truly hopeful for the future.

I hung up, grateful for her call, especially grateful for her news. The Christmas season had truly arrived!

But, that wasn't yet the rest of the story. Thirty days later, probably to the minute, the telephone rang again. This time the connection was better and the voice was stronger and more confident, *"Brother Hamilton, guess what? I have now been dry for two months. And guess what? The church can't find my records, and I get to be baptized again on Saturday."*

(Mormon doctrine requires baptism as a condition of membership in the church; and, if records are lost, then, baptism is again required as an assurance that the ordinance was actually done.)

In this instance there could have been no happier "accident" than the "loss" of her records—as the accomplishment anew of the ordinance would give her more of a tangible affirmation of the forgiveness of her past sins. Her excitement reflected this recognition.

She continued, *"And guess what? The kids have been going to church with me. And guess what? We are going back to court in a couple of weeks, and the social workers here think that I will get the kids back."*

Three weeks later, I heard from her again, *Brother Hamilton, they are home. I have my children back. And guess what? They have asked to be baptized this weekend!"*

That was the rest of the story.

* * *

Through all of this, *The Second Peter Principle* and Prescription touched and guided the course of several lives.

Personally, I was able to transcend the "me" that existed at the beginning of the relationship with the mother. Most importantly, I was able to recognize my own frailties and limitations in this situation, and I did submit to the disciplines of an orderly restructuring of "me."

I think, ultimately, I was able to show forth ". . . even charity." That is not to say that I have made "charity"—or even very many of the preceding steps "second nature" as yet.

However, I did re-enforce an earlier belief that, in such cases, there is a special dispensation that can allow us to transcend self. Great lessons were learned, and the next time will be easier.

* * *

As for the mother, great lessons were obviously learned as well. But, there were also great obstacles. There was a strong tendency on her part to superimpose her own demands for justice on top of the whole process. She slowly came to realize that her situation was not so incredibly unique. Many mothers who become dysfunctional by way of addictions, or abusive relationships, or whatever, are usually products of sexual abuse (incestuous or otherwise) that occurred in their youth. Understandably, this mother wanted restitution. She wanted to be back where she was—young, exuberant, and pure—before her step-father destroyed all that which was innocent and good. She wanted all that happened after to be magically erased. She, too, wanted a "special dispensation." And, for too long, she fought any suggestion that there was no magic answer.

Ultimately, she did come to the mature realization that life isn't always fair; some get dealt hands that are worse than others. You make the best of what you have, and you work through it—one step at a time, and in the order prescribed by Peter.

Later, she expressed the idea that, just maybe, there was a special dispensation after all—the arrival of a good road map and a capable tour guide.

* * *

Come to think about it, I really haven't told you the rest of the story. During the mother's last telephone call to me, she relayed one other small bit of news. It seems that her step-father, after all of these years had finally come to an honest recognition of what he had done. He was now in the process of trying to put things as right as he possibly could under the circumstances, and he had petitioned his church for permission to be re-baptized.

The really important part of this bit of news was the simple fact that this mother who had been so grievously wronged—and who had paid such a terrible price because of it, was now excited and rejoicing that another, who had fallen so far, could, likewise, pick himself up and seek to go forward, the right way.

This brings me to another discussion of "enemies." Unless we choose, professionally, to be attorneys, judges, or policemen, we probably go through life with few enemies—and few occasions to test our responses and to "grow" in this one area of unfamiliar terrain.

Again, I reiterate my personal belief in "special dispensations." Most of us have little opportunity to practice, to make second nature, our responses in hostile situations. However, if we have thought it out, if we truly accept the totality of the formula—and if we are diligently working on our growth in those areas where we can—then our appropriate responses as "enemies" will be almost automatic.

So it was with this mother. So it has been in my own life.

* * *

The juvenile court system is badly overworked and understaffed. Those who are involved can easily become jaded and cynical. Too often, there is a dreary sameness—a lack of change, lack of improvement, lack of success.

So, when a really dramatic turn-around takes place, it is noticed. And the real professionals, those who really care, look for explanations—look for ways of duplicating the process in the future.

Such was the case with this mother's court-appointed attorney. Early on, he too gave up on her. Sure, he continued to give her a "pro forma" sort of representation as a matter of legal necessity—but he had no hope that anything would ever change with her.

So, when the change was an established fact, when it had taken place so thoroughly and in such a short time, he began to ask questions.

He, too, now has *The Second Peter Principle* and Prescription. He has an intellectual understanding of the principles. He remains skeptical.

We continue to talk. I continue to work on "brotherly kindness." We'll see.

18 Repentance

Setting goals, and keeping on a path, consistently, to achieve them, is difficult to do. Some years ago, I set a goal of reading at least five pages of scriptures each day. I maintained that objective for a number of months. But the inevitable happened; one day I was unable to accomplish my reading. The next day, I was amazed at the difficulty that I was experiencing in getting back into my studies. My "perfect" record was destroyed. What was the point in continuing?

I had to quickly remind myself of the real reasons that I had set the goal, and those reasons had nothing to do with setting "perfect" records. I also realized that it would probably be extremely practical if I were to create an escape clause—that is, if I were to create a mechanism or a formula that would permit me to make up for days where I missed my reading for whatever reason. Since I have done that, daily scripture study has more truly become a habit with me.

It is the same way with *The Second Peter Principle.* It is not the end of the world if there is a day, for whatever reason, that I do not further the development of "me" in accordance with my long-term goals. But I pick it up the next day and go on from there.

I have discovered, however, that there is a more serious impediment to my progression towards moral perfection. In one of my roles, for example, I might be working on godliness or brotherly kindness—and then discover, very much to my chagrin, that I have done something really stupid, something that could call into question a virtue as basic as virtue itself in that same role.

In those circumstances, there may be feelings of, "What's the use? I'll never be able to do this!" Or, there may be feelings of great guilt. Such feelings, while understandable, are not productive unless they prompt corrective action. So there needs to be a mechanism to get things back on track—to restore things, as much as possible, as they were.

That process is called repentance. Properly done, the process overcomes the negative and unproductive feelings. It eliminates guilt. It restores things as they were.

The first step in the process is an honest recognition of what you have done. An honest recognition has no room for rationalizations—no room for calling a pound an ounce. An example of this is found in the fifty-first Psalm. David, feeling great remorse and guilt, plead to God for forgiveness saying, *Against thee, thee only have I sinned . . .* " David was in difficult straits because he had an affair with Bathsheba, had caused her to become pregnant. And because, in an attempt to hide his sin and his guilt, he sent Bathsheba's husband, Uriah, off to battle in such a way as to assure that he would be killed. David's remorse was real. But he was not honest in acknowledging the true nature of his actions.

The second step is determining, with real intent, to not do it again. Or, in the case of sins of omission, to determine to do what should have been done in the first place.

The next step is the really tough one. We need to face those whom we have wronged—privately, if we offended in private, but publicly if we offended in public. We need to confess what we have done.

We need to make restitution to the extent possible.

We need to ask forgiveness for what we have done. It is important to note here that we do not have to find forgiveness, we need only to ask. That is all that we can do. The individual whom we have offended might be of a disposition to withhold forgiveness, to seek revenge, or whatever. If that is the case, that is his problem.

Finally, we need to forgive ourselves. When we have taken all of the preceding steps, we need to be able to say, in effect: I wish I hadn't done it, but I did; I did everything that I could possibly do to correct it; I am not going to make that mistake again.

And when you've forgiven yourself, then it's time to put the situation behind you and get on with the important work of building a better and more perfect you.

One more comment seems appropriate at this point. Some churches might teach that there is more to the process of repentance; others teach that there is less. I wish not to get into a sectarian digression. What I have presented here is a commonsense synopsis of what I see as the essence of the scriptural teachings on the subject. I would not want my comments to detract from the teachings of your church that more may be required.

19
Conclusion

This is a small book. It is not intended as a scholarly commentary on a few verses in Second Peter. It is not intended to convey a message that moral perfection can be achieved by simply checking a few boxes on a special form.

It is my way of saying that I have a clear recognition that I am an imperfect being. I live in an imperfect world. I am not happy with either situation; I would change both.

I believe, too, that I am not alone in these feelings. I believe that such feelings stretch back at least two thousand years to the time of Peter. I believe that Peter recognized these same feelings in the people of his time, and that he was inspired as he penned these few verses.

I believe that his formula worked then, that it works now, that it will work tomorrow. I believe that the only real way that I can restructure "me" is through the adherence to these principles. I can change myself. I can change the world. I have come to realize that, if I follow this principle, step by step, I can accomplish the goal.

May you, likewise, come to the same realization.

> *May these things be in us and abound, may they make us that we shall neither be barren nor unfruitful in the knowledge of our Lord Jesus Christ.*

References

As I have written this little book, I have cited or referenced various individuals or works. Those sources are listed below, and for the most part, the broader and fuller reading will prove beneficial.

The Peter Principle by Laurence F. Peter & Raymond Hull, William Morrow & Company, Inc, New York, 1969.

The Road Less Travelled by M. Scott Peck, M.D., Simon & Schuster, New York, 1978.

People of the Lie by M. Scott Peck, M.D., Simon & Schuster, New York, 1983.

The Glory of God is Intelligence by Jacob Neusner, Publishers Press, Salt Lake City, 1978.

The Mask of Sanity by Hervey Cleckley, M.D., New American Library, New York, 1982.

The Reformation by Will Durant, Simon & Schuster, New York, 1957.

Lectures on Faith by Joseph Smith, Deseret Press, Salt Lake City.

The Autobiography of Benjamin Franklin by Benjamin Franklin, from Harvard Classics, Vol. 1, P. F. Collier & Son Corporation, New York, 1937.

Plutarch's Lives—Dryden translation, from Harvard Classics, Vol. 12, P. F. Collier & Son Corporation, New York, 1937.